I Wonder What It's Like to Be a Bee

Erin M. Hovanec

The Rosen Publishing Group's

PowerKids Press™

New York

To my grandfather, Jerry Conway, who gives new meaning to the phrase "busy as a bee" but is always there when I need him.

Published in 2000 by The Rosen Publishing Group, Inc.
29 East 21st Street, New York, NY 10010

Photo Credits: p. 4 © Animals, Animals/Stephen Dalton; p. 5 © CORBIS; p. 7 © Animals, Animals/Bill Beatty, © Animals, Animals/Stan Schroeder, © David Liebman; p. 8 © FPG/Jim Cumins; p. 9 © FPG/Geo Hagel Sr.; p. 11 © FPG/Stan Osolinski; p. 12 © Animals, Animals/Raymond A. Mendez, © Animals, Animals/Ken G. Preston, © Animals, Animals/Raymond A. Mendez; p.15 © Animals, Animals/Donald Specker ; p.16 © FPG/Gail Shumway; p. 17 © Animals, Animals/Zig Leszczynski; p. 19 © Hans Pfletschinger/Peter Arnold, Inc., © FPG/Larry West; p. 20 © James L. Amos/Peter Arnold, Inc.; p. 22 © CORBIS

Photo Illustrations by Thaddeus Harden

First Edition

Book Design: Felicity Erwin

Hovanec, Erin M.
    I wonder what it's like to be a bee / Erin Hovanec.
       p.   cm. — (Life science wonder series)
    Summary: Introduces the physical characteristics, habits, and behavior of bees.
    ISBN 0-8239-5450-1
    1.Bees Juvenile literature. [1. Bees.] I. Title. II. Series:
    Hovanec, Erin M. Life science wonder series.
    QL565.2.H68 1999
    595.79'9—dc21
                                                       99-29647
                                                         CIP

Manufactured in the United States of America

Contents

1 Just Buzzing Around 5

2 Yellow and Black, and Red and Green, Too! 6

3 Bees Are Beautiful 9

4 Pollen and Nectar 10

5 Home Sweet Home 13

6 Busy as a Bee 14

7 Danger! 17

8 Self-Defense 18

9 Dancing Bees 21

10 To Be a Bee 22

Glossary 23

Index 24

Web Sites 24

Just Buzzing Around

Have you ever wondered what it's like to be a bee, buzzing around all the time, eating honey and stinging people? It sounds like an easy life, doesn't it? Well, you may not know it, but there's a whole lot more to a bee's life than that.

Bees are important to plants, animals, and even people. Did you know that bees help plants **reproduce**? They also make the wax that humans use to make candles. Did you know that bees can dance? There's a lot most people don't know about what it's like to be a bee.

◀ *Bees don't just fly around. They work hard making wax and honey and finding food.*

Yellow and Black, and Red and Green, Too!

There are more than 20,000 **species** of bees. They live everywhere in the world except Antarctica. Most bees have short, thick bodies that are covered with hair.

The most common bees have yellow and black stripes on their bodies. You've probably seen these while you were at the park or in your backyard. Other bees have blue, brown, or green bodies. Some even have bright red or deep purple markings. Can you picture yourself with purple hair?

Different bees are different colors, but the most ▶ common are the yellow and black bees.

7

8

Bees Are Beautiful

What if you could smell everything you touched? Sounds strange, huh? If you were a bee, that wouldn't seem weird at all. Bees smell with **antennae**, or feelers, which are on their heads. Bees also have a **proboscis** on their heads, which is like a tongue. They use their antennae, proboscis, and special sensors on their front legs to taste.

The middle part of a bee's body is called the **thorax**. Bees have six legs and two pairs of wings attached to the thorax. Bees also have an **abdomen** behind the thorax, which holds many important organs that they need to reproduce and to **digest** their food.

◀ *Bees use their antennae to feel, smell, and taste. That's like having your hands, nose, and tongue all in one!*

Pollen and Nectar

Bees spend their days flying from flower to flower in search of a liquid called nectar. Nectar is sweet, sugary, and very tasty. Bees eat it or use it to make honey. As the bees are busy gathering nectar, the flower's **pollen**, or tiny seeds, sticks to their bodies. Flowers need pollen from other flowers to reproduce. When the bee is done snacking on one flower, it flies to another. Some of the pollen sticks to the bee's body and stays there until it is brushed off by the next flower. When a bee leaves pollen from one flower in another flower, it is called **pollination**. The bee is having a snack and enjoying the flowers, but it's also doing a very important job.

Bees aren't just relaxing when they visit a flower. They've got work to do.

Some solitary bees live in mud nests.

Parasitic bees use other bees to stay alive.

Honeybees live in group nests called colonies.

Home Sweet Home

Do you have your own room at home? Even if you share a room, you've probably found a private spot that's just for you. Everyone likes to be alone sometimes. Bees can be the same way. Most bees don't live in a nest or **hive**. Instead, they are **solitary**, or alone. Solitary bees build their own nests and care only for themselves and their young. Other bees are **parasitic**. Parasitic bees use other bees to help them stay alive. They leave their eggs in other bees' nests, hoping those bees will feed their young.

Social bees, like the ones you've probably seen, like being together. They live with other bees in hives or nests called **colonies**. Colonies can have as few as 10 bees or as many as 80,000 bees. That's a very big family!

◀ *Some bees like to live alone, while others live in groups. Can you imagine sharing a house with 80,000 people?*

Busy as a Bee

Have you ever heard the phrase, "busy as a bee"? Well, we say that because bees are always working to find honey and keep their houses in good shape. Social bees live in a hive, which is a nest with spaces to store honey. Bees store honey in six-sided spaces called **cells**. Honeybees save honey to eat during the winter, when the flowers are dead. The walls of a hive are made of beeswax, which bees make inside their bodies. The hive's most important bee is the queen. She is the biggest bee in the colony, and her only job is to have babies. She has the babies by **mating** with the male bees, called drone bees. Most of the bees in the colony are worker bees. Workers are small female bees. They gather nectar for food and feed the queen. They also build and guard the colony and care for the colony's young.

The cell walls in a hive can hold 25 times their own weight ▶ without breaking!

Danger!

You may be scared of bees, but bees are probably scared of you, too. Bees have lots of enemies. They are **prey** for many animals. Prey are animals that are hunted by other animals for food. Skunks sometimes wait outside bees' nests and eat bees that leave. Bears like to eat bees, too, and often destroy entire nests. Hungry mice also enter nests during the winter, when the bees are all inside. They eat the bees and even the nests. Sometimes bees are even preyed upon by other bees. One group of bees may attack and kill another to steal their honey.

Unlike many other insects, most bees are not **predators**. Predators are animals that live by eating or attacking other animals. Bees are peaceful insects. They only eat nectar, which they get from flowers.

◀ *Bees sometimes attack bees' nests in search of honey.*

Self-Defense

Have you ever been stung by a bee? That's no fun for you, but it's the way some bees protect themselves from danger. Many bees have small **stingers**. Most bees can sting many times, but a honeybee will die after stinging only once. Stingless bees defend their colonies by crawling into an animal's eyes, ears, and nose. They will also climb under a human's clothing. Some even give off a **chemical** that burns the skin.

The most dangerous bees release a chemical into the air when they are in danger. This chemical tells other bees to join them, and then the bees swarm their attacker in great numbers. These bees have killed large animals and even humans.

Bees have to protect themselves against ▶
invaders and predators.

Honey bees guard the entrance to their hive against predators.

Killer bees swarm when they are in danger.

19

Dancing Bees

Can you imagine only being able to tell someone something by dancing? For us that would be hard, but for a bee it's natural. When a worker bee finds food, she goes back to the hive. First she gives the other bees a taste of the nectar. From its taste and smell, the other bees know what kind of food she has found. The worker then tells them where to find the food by dancing.

The other worker bees can tell the honeybees how far away the food is by the speed and length of her dance. They can also tell which direction it's in by the way she points her tail. If the worker has found lots of food, she dances with more energy and excitement. She wants everyone to share in her good luck.

◀ *The bees in this picture are doing what scientists call the "waggle dance." They are telling other bees where to find food.*

To Be a Bee

What would it be like to be a bee? You'd spend lots of time snacking and helping plants and flowers grow. You'd have colorful hair all over your body and antennae on your head. You could sting all your enemies. You could make honey and wax inside your body. You'd even get to dance! It wouldn't be bad to be a bee, would it?

Glossary

abdomen (AB-doh-min) The third section of an insect's body, which contains many important body parts.

antennae (an-TEN-uh) Feelers that bees use to feel, smell, and taste.

cells (SELZ) The sections in a hive where bees store honey.

chemical (KEM-ih-kuhl) A specific substance.

colonies (KAH-luh-neez) The nest of social bees.

digest (dy-JEST) To break up food so the body can use it.

hive (HYV) A nest with space to store honey.

mating (MAYT-ing) When a male body and female body join in a special way to produce offspring.

parasitic (pahr-uh-SIT-ik) An animal that depends on another animal to live.

pollen (PAH-lin) A fine, yellowish powder needed to fertilize flowers and plants.

pollination (pah-lih-NAY-shun) When an animal, water, or wind moves tiny bits of pollen from one flower to another.

predators (PREH-da-torz) Animals that live by eating or attacking other animals.

prey (PRAY) Animals that are eaten or attacked by other animals.

proboscis (proh-BIHS-kus) A tongue-like organ used to taste.

reproduce (ree-PROH-doos) To make more of something.

solitary (SAHL-ih-teh-ree) Alone.

species (spee-SEES) A category of animals which have many things in common.

stingers (STING-erz) Pointed objects on bees that sting painfully.

thorax (THOR-ax) The center section of an insect's body.

Index

A
abdomen, 9
antennae, 9, 22

C
colonies, 13, 14, 18

D
digest, 9
drone bees, 14

E
enemies, 17, 22

F
flowers, 10, 14, 17, 22

H
hive, 13, 14, 21
honey, 5, 10, 14, 17, 22
honeybees, 14, 18, 21

N
nectar, 10, 14, 17, 21
nests, 13, 14, 17

P
parasitic, 13
pollen, 10
pollination, 10
predators, 17
prey, 17
proboscis, 9

Q
queen bee, 14

R
reproduce, 5, 9, 10

S
social bees, 13, 14
solitary, 13
species, 6

T
thorax, 9

W
wax, 5, 14, 22
worker bees, 14, 21

Web Sites

You can learn more about bees on the Internet.
Check out this Web site:
http://gears.tucson.ars.ag.gov/